DWAYNE J

A Little Golden Book® Biography

By Frank Berrios
Illustrated by Irene Chan

A GOLDEN BOOK • NEW YORK

Text copyright © 2023 by Frank Berrios
Cover art and interior illustrations copyright © 2023 by Irene Chan
All rights reserved. Published in the United States by Golden Books, an imprint of
Random House Children's Books, a division of Penguin Random House LLC, 1745 Broadway,
New York, NY 10019. Golden Books, A Golden Book, A Little Golden Book, the G colophon,
and the distinctive gold spine are registered trademarks of Penguin Random House LLC.
rhcbooks.com
Educators and librarians, for a variety of teaching tools, visit us at RHTeachersLibrarians.com
Library of Congress Control Number: 2021947496
ISBN 978-0-593-48548-4 (trade) — ISBN 978-0-593-48549-1 (ebook)
Printed in the United States of America
10 9 8 7 6 5 4 3 2 1

Dwayne Douglas Johnson was born in Hayward, California, on May 2, 1972. His mother, Ata Johnson, was the daughter of "High Chief" Peter Maivia, a Samoan American wrestler and promoter. Dwayne's father, "Soul Man" Rocky Johnson, was also a talented wrestler.

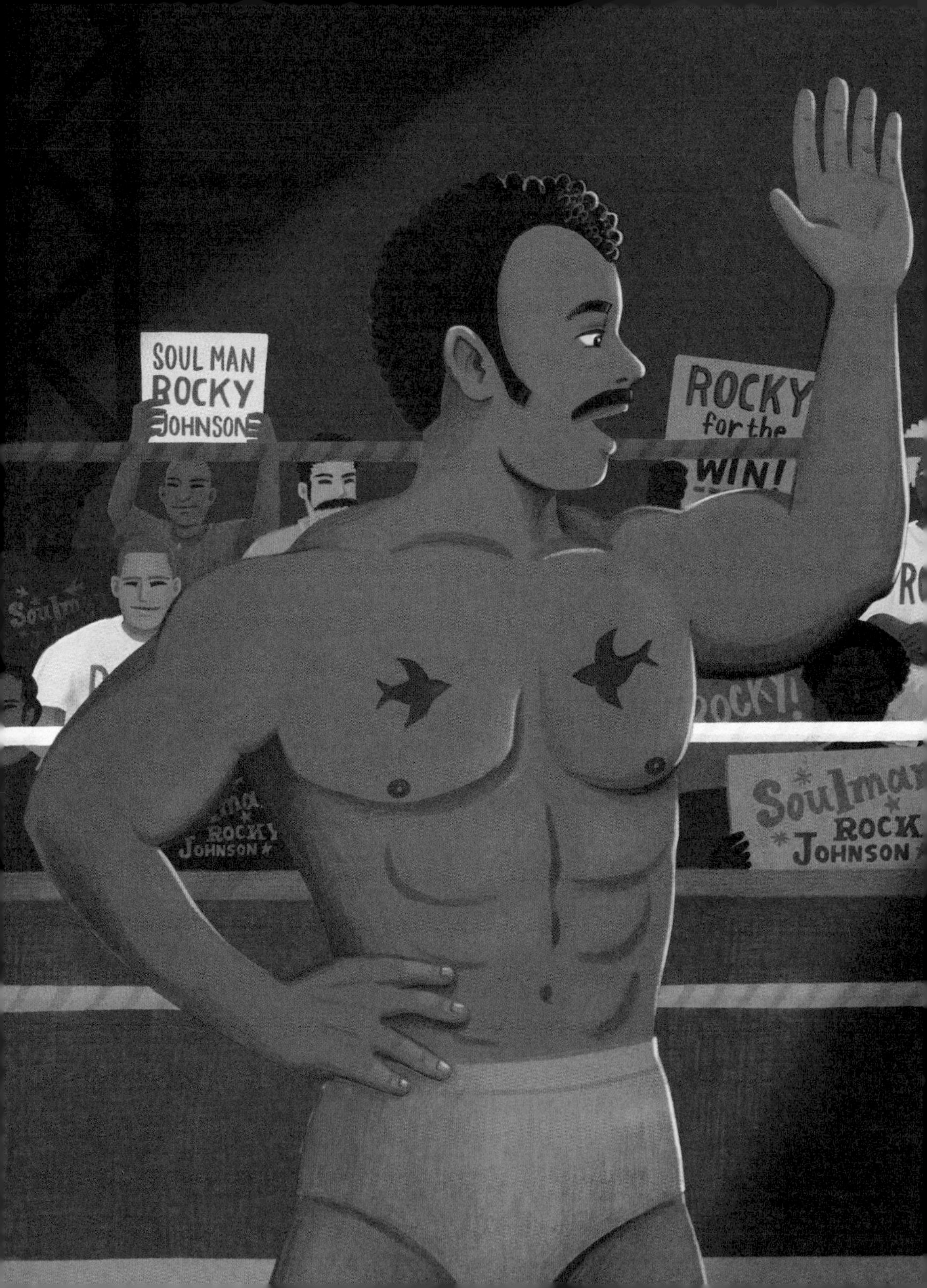
SOUL MAN
ROCKY
JOHNSON
ROCKY
for the
WIN!

Dwayne, or Dewey, as he was known back then, loved to watch his father wrestle. His dad was handsome, smart, and strong. Plus, he had lots of fans!

Dwayne's grandmother, Lia Maivia, was one of the first female wrestling promoters in Hawaii. As a result, Dwayne grew up surrounded by amazing wrestlers, including the Wild Samoans, Junkyard Dog, the Iron Sheik . . .

THE WILD SAMOANS

Growing up with a dad who was a famous wrestler was fun, but life wasn't always easy. The family moved often to follow his father's wrestling career. And as the new kid in school, Dwayne would sometimes get into fights with bullies.

Dwayne's parents didn't always have enough money to buy him the things he wanted. When he was a teenager, Dwayne got in trouble for stealing sneakers and clothes.

Thankfully, his parents kept him focused on doing well in school and working hard.

Dwayne was much bigger and faster than most kids his age, so when he started to play football in high school, he quickly became the best player on the team.

Dwayne graduated from high school in 1990 and earned a football scholarship from the University of Miami. He was proud to be the first person in his family to go to college. But after getting injured during practice, he was unable to play his entire first year. Dwayne was heartbroken, and thought about dropping out of school.

Everything seemed to change when Dwayne met a fellow student named Dany Garcia. For him, it was love at first sight! Dany inspired Dwayne to study and get better grades. Two years after he graduated from college, he and Dany got married.

Dwayne dreamed of becoming a football player after school. Unfortunately, he wasn't selected to play for any professional teams. Dwayne was upset, but he didn't let this setback get him down. He decided to have his dad train him for the family business: wrestling!

Dwayne made his professional wrestling debut in 1996 under the ring name Rocky Maivia. The name was a tribute to his dad, Rocky Johnson, and his grandfather, Peter Maivia.

Dwayne was nervous about wrestling in front of thousands of screaming fans in New York City. But the energy from the crowd helped lead him to an amazing victory!

A good guy in wrestling is known as a babyface, or a face. Dwayne would go on to become the Intercontinental Champion of the World Wrestling Federation (WWF) as a face. But after a small wrestling injury, he returned to the ring with a new name and a new attitude. From then on, he was known simply as . . .

. . . the Rock!

Bad guys, or heels, as they are called in wrestling, are often popular. Fans couldn't get enough of the Rock. They loved his bold behavior and were tickled by his catchphrase "Can you smell what the Rock is cooking?" He also liked to be called the People's Champion and the Great One.

The Rock faced off against wrestling icons, such as Hulk Hogan and John Cena.

As an eight-time World Wrestling Entertainment (WWE) Champion, the Rock proved time and again that he was the most electrifying man in sports entertainment!

Dwayne enjoyed wrestling, but he also wanted to act. In 2001, the same year he and Dany welcomed a daughter, Simone, Dwayne made his big-screen debut in *The Mummy Returns.* His work on that project led to a role in another movie, *The Scorpion King.*

Dwayne worked just as hard in Hollywood as he had on the football field and in the wrestling ring. He took small roles and met with acting coaches to improve his skills. He has been in everything from action films to comedies to kids' movies. He even has a star on the Hollywood Walk of Fame!

PRODUCTION

Dwayne is also a talented voice actor and singer. Maui, Dwayne's character in Disney's *Moana,* was inspired by his grandfather, Peter Maivia. In the film, Dwayne's character sings a song called "You're Welcome."

After eleven years, Dwayne and Dany decided to end their marriage, but not their friendship. They still work together. Their company, Seven Bucks Productions, creates television shows and movies for kids and adults.

In 2019, Dwayne married Lauren Hashian in a beautiful ceremony in Hawaii. The couple has two daughters, Jasmine and Tiana.

When Dwayne isn't working, or working out, he enjoys fishing and spending time with his family.

Dwayne Johnson is one of the greatest wrestlers ever. He made the incredible leap from the ring to Hollywood and has been in more than thirty blockbuster films. With his amazing talent and drive, there's no telling what he'll do next!